Corbridge Roman Site
NORTHUMBERLAND

J N DORE

The Roman site at Corbridge was strategically placed at the intersection of one of the principal routes into Scotland and a line of communication between the Tyne and the Solway. It was therefore the site of a series of military forts which began in the last quarter of the first century and continued until shortly after the middle of the second. Though lying behind the line of Hadrian's Wall, it probably continued to play a support role throughout the period.

In about AD165, a new arrangement for a garrison town began to take shape on the site of the fort, and this flourished until at least the beginning of the fifth century. It is the remains from this later period which are mainly visible today, although the area now on view represents only the nucleus of the town itself, which covered a wide area. The museum contains a rich selection of finds from the whole area.

ENGLISH HERITAGE · LONDON

CONTENTS

3	TOUR	29	THE MUSEUM
3	Museum	29	Note on dating
3	The main street	31	History
5	Buildings north of the main street	31	*The Agricolan supply base at Red House*
5	*Granaries*		
7	*Fountain house and aqueduct*	31	*The forts at Corbridge I*
8	*Site 11*	31	*The Corbridge hoard*
11	Buildings south of the main street	31	*The forts at Corbridge II*
12	*The east compound*	32	*The forts at Corbridge III*
14	*The side street*	32	*Inscriptions and sculpture*
14	*The west compound*	34	*The later military occupation*
		34	*The Corbridge lion*
18	HISTORY	34	Life in Roman Corbridge
18	The name of Roman Corbridge	34	*Personal effects*
18	The first settlers	34	*Building in the Roman town*
18	Red House Fort	35	*Local industry and pottery*
18	The forts at Corbridge	35	*Glass*
18	*The earliest fort*	36	*Domestic life*
19	*The second fort*	37	*Imports to Corbridge*
22	*The third fort and Hadrian's Wall*	38	*Agriculture and trade*
22	*The last fort*	38	*Religion*
22	*The end of the forts*	39	*Death*
22	Development of the town		
23	*Early development*		
26	*The third and fourth centuries*		
27	Corbridge after the Romans		
28	Rediscovery and excavation		

Unless otherwise stated illustrations are copyright English Heritage and the photographs were taken by the English Heritage Photographic Section

Published by English Heritage
1 Waterhouse Square, 138–142 Holborn, London EC1N 2ST
© Copyright English Heritage 1989
First published 1989, reprinted 1991, 1993, 1995, 1997, 1998, 2000, 2001, 2008, 2010, 2013
Revised reprint 2012
Printed in England by Pureprint Group
11/13, C30, 04080
ISBN 978 1 85074 247 0

TOUR

Museum

The area of remains visible today at Corbridge and in the care of English Heritage represents only a small fraction of what was once clearly a major Roman town. Many more buildings have been excavated in the surrounding area, including baths, shops and houses, covering an area of about 27 acres (11ha). The site museum contains some of the wealth of material found during excavation, and it is recommended that you visit the museum before viewing the remains. A detailed description of the material on display in the museum will be found on page 29.

On leaving the museum, you should turn right along the side of the two buttressed granaries, and then left on to what was the main street of the Roman town.

The main street

The main street of the Roman town runs from east to west through the middle of the site. To its north (left) lie a pair of granaries, a fountain house and a large courtyard building, known for convenience as Site 11, the number given it during the excavations in 1908. To the south are two enclosed compounds.

At its highest points, by the granaries and by the east fence of the site, the top surface of the street is of fourth-century date. Towards the centre of the site much of this top surface was removed during early excavations as it contained many pieces of re-used sculpture, and the visible surface here probably dates from the third century. Beneath these surfaces are layer upon layer of earlier road metalling which go down for several metres and trace the history of the site back through the earlier phases of the town and the preceding forts to the first street, which was probably laid down around AD90. In the middle of the site, opposite Site 11, the main street is joined from the south (right) by a side street. This too, lies over a succession of earlier streets which extend back to the early forts.

The main street continues under the fields both east and west of the remains visible today. Excavations early this century showed that it was lined with rectangular buildings. Just east of the boundary of the area open to visitors it was joined from the north by a street forming part of the Roman Dere Street which ran north into Scotland and south to London. To the west it was joined, some 80 metres west of the museum, by the road from the Roman bridge over the Tyne. Further west the line of the street is soon lost, although it is presumed that it once ran all the way to Carlisle, forming part of the Roman road known as the Stanegate.

Although their position is not known with any certainty the cemeteries of the town would have been situated outside its limits by the side of the roads. A mausoleum (monumental tomb), which was once marked by a sculpture of a lion and stag similar to the one on display in the museum, was excavated on Shorden Brae to the west of the town. A number of inscribed tombstones which must have come from one of the cemetery areas were re-used in late levels on the site and some are on display in the museum.

4 TOUR: Plan of north side of street

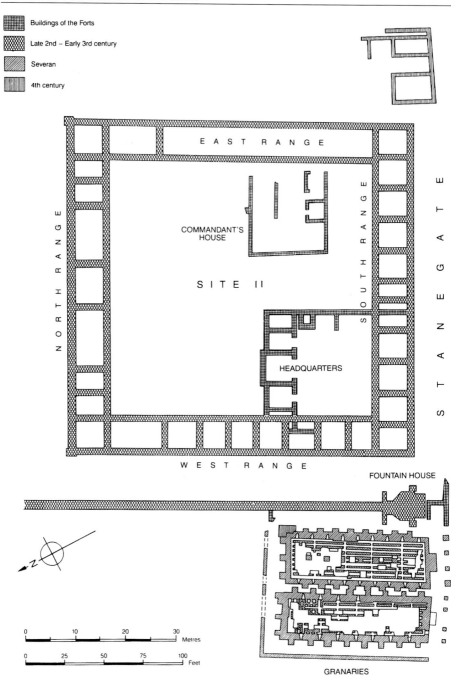

Buildings north of the main street

Buildings north of the main street

Granaries

These two buildings were designed to store large quantities of grain for long periods. A good circulation of air kept the grain cool and dry. To do this the floors were supported on low stone sleeper walls (which can be seen below the flagged floors in both buildings) and the interior both above and below the floors was ventilated. Low down, between the buttresses of the main walls, was a series of narrow vents connected to the underfloor space. Many of these vents can be seen in the main walls: a stone mullion occurs at the south end of the east side of the east granary. Set higher up in the walls would have been large louvred wooden shutters to keep air circulating. Both buildings were surrounded by a stone-lined drain to combat damp conditions, and by an enclosure wall.

At the south (street) end were the entrances, each with a loading platform (only that of the east granary now remains) and sheltered from the elements by porticoes (porches) whose columns stand beside the road. Just by the entrance to the west granary can be seen a small opening to the underfloor space. An interesting detail is hard to find: where the lowest floor of the west granary joins its north wall there is an upside-down incised carving of a temple with a triangular pediment and four pillars. Running down the middle of the east granary was a row of columns whose bases can be seen set in the floor; it is possible that this granary had two storeys and the columns supported the upper floor.

The granaries looking south, with the west granary in the foreground and the east granary to the left. The stone-flagged floor of the west granary is the best preserved. Down the centre of the east granary are square bases for columns, which may have supported an upper floor

6 TOUR: Granaries

This stone mullion in a vent in the south-east corner of the east granary is the only one surviving in situ *in Britain*

bottom of a set of steps which leads down into the building from the entrance rests on one of the earlier sleeper walls. This interruption is thought to have been caused by an invasion of the province by hostile tribes from north of Hadrian's Wall, which is known to have taken place in AD180. The buildings were probably completed in the early third century.

The granaries remained in use throughout the third century and into the fourth. A hoard of coins which was probably deposited around the middle of the fourth century was found on the loading platform of the east granary. The last resurfacing of the road took place some time after AD364. This raised the level outside the granary portico to its present position. Large stone slabs (no longer visible) had to be placed between the columns and the road material to stop it slipping into the portico, and a set of

The construction of the granaries began about AD180 but certain features suggest that the work was interrupted for a time and then resumed. Different styles of work can be detected in the main walls of both buildings, and in the porticoes three different kinds and sizes of column were used: those for the west granary are all the same, but the outer pair for the east granary are different and the inner pair different again. More of the west granary had been built when the interruption occurred and it had to be quite extensively modified before it was finished. It has two sets of sleeper walls below floor level, one built on top of the other; the gaps between the lower sets of walls were filled in with cobbles and clay before the upper set was built; and the

The bases of the columns of the porticoes which once sheltered the loading bays. This clearly shows how the street level was raised through resurfacing after the granaries had been built

The granaries and fountain house, looking east, with the main street on the right. At the top of the picture can be seen the course of the aqueduct bringing water to the fountain house (top right)

stone steps (also no longer visible) was provided between the westernmost pair of columns to enable people to reach the floor of the portico. How long the buildings remained in use after this is uncertain.

To the north of the east granary is a small rectangular building. Its use is not known but inside, in 1908, a hoard of forty-eight gold solidi (fourth-century coins) was found. The date of the latest coin showed that the hoard must have been deposited some time after AD383.

Fountain house and aqueduct
To the east of the granaries, at the centre of the town, was the main distribution point for the public water supply.

The water was brought into the site from the north. (Close by the hedge at this side can be seen the channelled stone blocks of the conduit together with their capping stones.) The aqueduct or conduit was carried on a bank of rubble and clay faced with masonry and would originally have been covered over with a lagging of clay and stones.

At the fountain house, the bank terminated against two short lengths of wall. Though it is no longer visible today, this is where the water would have flowed from the conduit through an ornamental spout into the aeration basin beyond. In the museum are two fragments of an ornamental triangular pediment which would have crowned this fountain head. The fragments are just big enough to show the design of the complete original: two winged Victories holding between them a corona (circular wreath) containing the words '*LEG XX VV FECIT*' (the Twentieth Legion, called Valeria Victrix, built this).

The water, which had flowed for quite

8 TOUR: Fountain house

Fragments of the stone pediment which once adorned the fountain house

some time in the closed conduit, needed to be allowed to mix with air to restore its freshness and this was the purpose of the aeration tank. This was a massive structure. Above the foundations are three courses of blocks which were held together with metal or wooden cramps, and which formed a polygonal base for a lead tank surrounded by a decorated stone screen. Neither the tank nor the screen survives today but the grooved blocks into which the screen fitted can be seen at the front of the stone base. On either side of the aeration tank are pedestals on which statues, probably of Victories, would have stood. In front of this, next to the road, is a large stone trough, into which the water flowed through spouts from the aeration tank. From the trough it could be drawn for public use, and years of wear from the overflow of water have left their mark on its sides. A drain in its south-west corner provided an outlet and channelled water from this and from the drain surrounding the granaries into the main drains from the street.

To judge by the various road levels it seems that the building of this public water supply started at the same time as the granaries and the building known as Site 11. The visible trough was not the original one, however; below its west end can be seen protruding the floor of an earlier trough which was probably linked with the outfall drain at its south-east end. The statue bases also may have been later additions.

At the time that the water supply was in use the road would have extended right up to the trough. Modern excavation has enabled us today to see the drains in front of it which connect with a system of tanks in the compounds on the south side of the street. Also exposed at the same level as these drains is the south-west corner of a stone building belonging to one of the series of earlier forts which lie under the surface of the site. The building was a workshop and was probably built around AD140.

Site 11 (forum/storehouse)

Beyond the fountain house on the north side of the street, and extending almost to the site boundaries, are the remains of a large courtyard building, known as Site 11. Its function is open to interpretation.

TOUR: Fountain house 9

Top: A reconstruction drawing of the fountain house, with the stone trough in the foreground. The photograph shows the remains today from the same angle: the trough and statue base can be clearly made out

When it was first discovered, it was thought to be a forum, because it was similar in shape and size to those of other Roman towns. The combination of a forum and basilica (a large hall) usually formed the central civic building in a Roman town. Later excavators thought that it was more likely to have been a storehouse, forming part of a military depot, and more recently the suggestion has been made that it could have been a market.

The building is square in shape with four ranges of rooms surrounding a central courtyard. Today, little survives apart from the foundations; only in places do one or two courses of the main walls still stand. The little that remains, however, is enough to show the quality of craftsmanship which originally went into it. The site was carefully levelled and the building properly laid out; the foundations were securely bedded and the stone blocks accurately cut and jointed. There are good reasons, however, for thinking that the building was never completed. The foundations of the far north range appear never to have had any stonework laid upon them, and walls at the north end of both the east and west ranges can never have been built to their full height because the upper surfaces of the topmost blocks had never been dressed level.

The main entrance to the building is thought to have been in the centre of the south range. Under the roadway running through the entrance can be seen a large stone drain. At the west end of the south range, facing on to the street, the pillar bases for a portico can still be seen. Overlying the east end of the range fragments of a later building have been found.

The north, west and south ranges were divided into a number of rooms. The surviving fragments of walling at the south end of the west range suggest that the rooms here may have had arched openings facing on to the courtyard. The east range contains a long, single undivided room.

The building of Site 11 is thought to have started some time around AD 180. Though the whole building may never have been completed, the south range and part of the west range seem to have been sufficiently finished to have been used. In these rooms, archaeologists found two, and sometimes three, superimposed floor levels, and evidence which suggested that both ranges were in use in the third century, but that by the fourth century only three rooms of the south range were still being used. In one of these rooms a hoard of four hundred coins was found under the topmost floor; they were deposited at around the middle of the fourth century.

The reason the building was never finished was probably the serious unrest in the province which occurred towards the end of the second century AD. There is evidence of fire at about this time in a number of places at Corbridge, though whether this was the result of direct enemy action or organised Roman withdrawal is uncertain.

Earlier buildings In the courtyard can be seen the remains of two earlier buildings. Both belong to one of the series of forts of which the remains lie beneath the site. The building on the west was a headquarters building; that on the east a commanding officer's house. The layout of headquarters buildings in Roman forts followed a relatively standard pattern: at the front of the building was a courtyard surrounded by a portico, at the back were a number of small offices on either side of a shrine room *(aedes)* where the regimental standards were kept, and in the middle

The south side of Site 11, looking north west towards the museum. This range clearly contained a number of rooms, and the main entrance was probably at its centre

was a long hall. The visible remains of the headquarters building formed part of the offices and shrine. The small square room was the shrine, and between this and the west range of the courtyard building can be seen the remains of one of the offices. Most of the rest of the building lies buried.

The fact that these fragments of earlier buildings were never removed prior to the courtyard being levelled at the time when Site 11 was being built is another good reason for thinking that the building was never finished.

Immediately to the east of Site 11, at the far end of the main street, are the remains of a small building of unknown function. To judge from its level, which is considerably higher than Site 11, it probably dates to the third or fourth centuries.

Buildings south of the main street

The undulations across the southern part of the site are caused by subsidence over the ditches of one of the earliest forts.

Most of the buildings on the south side of the main street are contained within two walled compounds, whose character is likely to have been military. However, a number of buildings facing directly on to the main street are not contained within the compounds, and pre-date the building of the compound walls. The best preserved is where you are now standing, at the far east end of

12   TOUR: The east compound

Reconstruction drawing showing, on the left, two of the buildings facing on to the main street, outside the east compound. These were probably temples. Next to them is a side gate to the east compound

the site, and the arrangement at the north-west corner of the east compound suggests that there was once one here also. There are remains of two others to the north-west of the west compound. Some of them may have supported columns and may have been temples, although it has been argued that the temple precinct could have been elsewhere, and that these may simply have been storehouses.

The east compound
Enter the east compound at the south-east corner. The remains of many of the buildings here are very fragmentary and survive only as clay and cobble foundations; at this end of the compound are several buildings of which the remains are too elusive to give much clue as to their function. A small square building might have been a latrine. It has been suggested that the two buildings against the compound wall were meeting rooms (*scholae*) for the social and welfare clubs (*collegia*) for lower ranking soldiers. This is open to question, as is the suggestion that the building which faces the entrance to the compound was a headquarters. It bears a superficial resemblance, with its small apse, to that

of the west compound, and is situated in a corresponding position.
  Beyond these buildings are some fragments of what may have been residential accommodation. On the right is a small building which judging from its contents (several hearths and furnaces) was probably used as a workshop, and further on is a larger building with a regular arrangement which suggests that it was a barrack block.
  At the west end of the compound right of the main entrance are the superimposed remains of a series of residential houses, the most substantial remains within the compound. The earliest remains are of two square buildings of very similar plan, consisting of a number of rooms grouped round a central courtyard. They were probably the residences of the officers in charge of the legionaries who formed the garrison of the compounds. Subsequent modifications have obscured many of the details but some of the entrances to the rooms can still be made out. The entrance to the northern building was on its east side, while that of the south building was from the street just inside the compound gate. A drain which can be seen flowing through several of the rooms

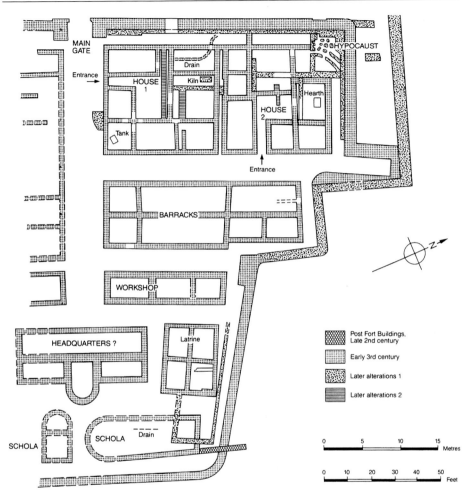

Buildings of the east compound

on the west side of the south house and out under its west wall at the north-west corner indicates that there was probably a latrine in one of these rooms.

Subsequent modifications turned the two buildings into one larger one, and probably involved their almost complete rebuilding. The new buildings re-used parts of the east sides of the previous buildings, but had new work on the west and north sides. Here it was extended as far as was practicable, and its new walls

lined the inner face of the main north compound wall. This was later removed so that today one can see the rough core of the walls of the enlarged house, abutting the compound wall. In the north-west corner room of the enlarged house a hypocaust (underfloor heating system) was installed and in the rooms adjoining this can be seen the check stones of the door thresholds.

Either at this time or later a potter's kiln was installed in one of the rooms in

14 TOUR: The side street

The remains of a hypocaust in the north-west corner of the house in the east compound

the southern half of the building. In the next but one room to the east of the kiln, two tanks were found full of unworked potting clay. Judging from the large amounts of waste pottery found in the surrounding area the most popular type of vessel manufactured in the kiln was a flat dish in coarse yellowish-red ware.

The side street

Emerging from the main entrance to the east compound you are now standing in the side street which divides the two compounds. The main entrances to the compounds lay near the south end of this street. The level of the street today is of the same date as the compound walls; a later resurfacing was removed during excavation. Across the north end of the side street can be seen the remains of a wall which was built in the third or fourth centuries to close off the street and unite the two compounds. The projections in this wall towards its west end probably formed the base for bastions or towers on either side of a gate. On the north side of the wall, just to the east of the projections, was found a coin hoard which was deposited at

around the middle of the fourth century.

On each side of the north end of the side street are stone water tanks which received their supply from a conduit running beneath the main street from the fountain house. Drains on either side of the side street carried any overflow southwards towards the river. One of the outfall drains for the west compound can be seen just to the north of the entrance as it runs through a fine arched conduit in the compound wall. Another runs through the gate of the compound.

The west compound

Temple Immediately inside the gate of the west compound to the right are the remains of a small building which was built before the compound wall but later incorporated into it. Its size and shape suggest that it was a temple. It was well built, with plastered inner faces to the walls and a small apse at its west end. Entrances can be detected in its remains at three places: the earliest was at the east end, and outside this can be seen four bases for the pillars of a small porch or

The arched conduit for a drain, north of the entrance to the west compound. This was part of the sophisticated water supply and drainage system of the fort

TOUR: The west compound   15

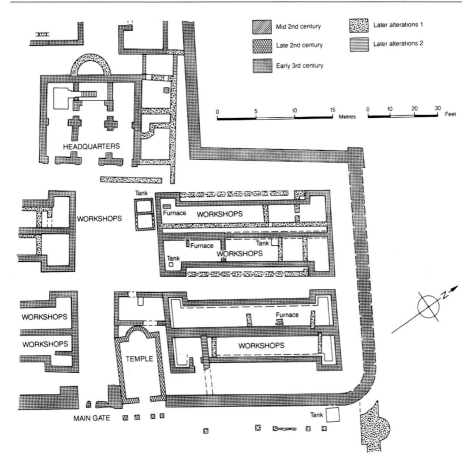

Buildings of the west compound

portico. The next entrance, probably inserted when the compound wall was built, was at the east end of the north wall, where the iron door pivot complete with its spindle was found; and the latest entrance was in the north-west corner. The building had two floor levels, the earlier associated with a curious system of multiple drains.

Workshops To the north and south of this small temple are the remains of four long buildings, all originally built to the same plan and thus probably having the

The temple inside the west compound, looking south east

TOUR: The west compound

same function. Each was divided in two down its length by a stone wall, and the long narrow rooms so formed have small projecting wings at either end. The positions of doorways suggest that both halves were divided in two again, probably by timber partitions. Inside the northern two buildings a series of hearths and tanks associated with iron slag were found, and from the western of the two came a deposit of iron spear- and arrow-heads. From this it is clear that the buildings were used as workshops at some time, though their plan suggests that they were not originally intended as such. Three of them underwent considerable modification during their lifetime and the iron-working may belong to the later phases.

Headquarters At the far, west end of the compound stands a building which was probably an administrative headquarters. The original building was roughly square in plan with an entrance in the main east wall. It was divided internally into six square rooms of roughly equal size. Remains of the foundations suggest that many of the interior walls were carried on arches across the openings between rooms. Under the southern room on the west side was a small underground chamber entered by a flight of steps from the room to the north. Similar rooms in headquarters buildings at Chesters and South Shields are thought to have been used as strong rooms. On the steps were found a large altar dedicated to the Imperial Discipline by the Second Legion and part of a building inscription dedicated by the Sixth Legion, which mentions an early third-century governor called Virius Lupus. Also found inside

The underground strong room in the headquarters building, looking north. The room at the top of the stairs would have been the shrine, the centre of religious life for the garrison

the building were a carved relief of Hercules brandishing a club, and a statue of a partly draped male figure, probably Jupiter. All these are on display in the museum. The last two items, together with the altar to the Imperial Discipline, suggest that the building was a headquarters and that the room at the head of the stairs was the shrine around which the religious life of the garrison centered.

A whole series of changes was later made to the headquarters building. First, a range of rooms was added on the north side. The middle room was probably a latrine and the one immediately to the west of it had plastered walls. Subsequently, a new entrance hall spanning the whole width of the building was added on the east front, and a small room containing a hypocaust was then added at the west end of the new north range, connecting it to an earlier building which lies behind. The hypocaust was renewed once and under the top floor was found a coin of Valentinian I, showing that it was still functioning in the late fourth century. Finally, the small gap between the hypocaust room and the compound wall was closed off. At some point also a small apse was added to the west wall of the building.

In the space in front of the headquarters stands the base of a large tank which was part of the water supply of the compound. The marks on it where the sides originally fitted show work of more than one period: it appears that an

The remains of the water tank outside the headquarters, which appears to have been extended at some point

original almost square tank was later extended. Both the drains coming from its east end are outlets: one flows out through the arched conduit in the compound wall and the other through the gate to join the drain on the west side of the south street. The tank could have been fed by rainwater from the roofs of the nearby buildings.

Returning to the museum between the remains of the workshops and the west compound wall you pass on your left the remains of two buildings which were probably temples (see page 12). Overlying the corner of one of these is a small building which is known as the 'pottery shop' from the quantity of pottery which has been found here. This seems to have been destroyed by fire in the late fourth century.

HISTORY

The name of Roman Corbridge

The name *Corstopitum* by which the site is often known today is derived from the Antonine Itinerary (an early third century collection of road routes in the Roman empire) but it is almost certainly corrupt. A similar name occurs in the Ravenna Cosmography, an eighth-century collection of place names. The original name cannot be restored with certainty but may have been something like *Coriosopitum*. *Corio-* was possibly the name for the centre of a Pagus (a subdivision of a Celtic tribal territory). The rest of the name may have referred to an actual tribe.

The first settlers

The Romans were not the first on the site. Beneath the courtyard of the large building known as Site 11 (from the site number given to it in the excavations of 1908) evidence of pre-Roman settlement has been found. Excavations revealed a shallow circular ditch enclosing six post-holes which may have belonged to a circular hut.

Red House Fort

The Romans first arrived in the Corbridge area in AD79. By this time the lowland areas of south-east Britain had been part of the Roman Empire for about thirty years. The force which arrived at Corbridge was part of an army commanded by the governor, Julius Agricola, which was advancing through northern England and into Scotland with the intention of extending Roman rule over the whole island. About half a mile to the west of the present site they built a large fort to supply the campaigning army as it moved deeper into enemy territory. It contained barracks, workshops and store buildings. Close by, they built a bath house for the use of the men who were stationed there. Both have been excavated, the fort in 1974 and the bath house between 1957 and 1959. They are known by the name of the modern farm, the Red House farm, which stands close by.

The forts at Corbridge

The earliest fort

Agricola and his army won a victory over the Scottish tribes in AD84 at a place called *Mons Graupius* (thought to be near modern Aberdeen). Soon afterwards, he was recalled to Rome, but the work of consolidating his victory was already under way. A legionary fortress (at Inchtuthil, near Perth) and a whole series of smaller forts were built to control the newly conquered areas and restrict the movement of hostile tribes. As part of this scheme, the Red House base was abandoned and a new fort built on the present Corbridge site.

Remains of this first fort have been found in the lowest levels of the excavations, though none of it is now visible today. Its rampart was built of turf and its gates and internal buildings of timber. At its north and south ends were barracks; the central area contained the headquarters, the commanding officer's residence, a workshop, accommodation for the administrative staff and a pair of granaries. Its garrison is thought to have been a unit of cavalry of five hundred men, called the Ala Petriana.

With certain minor modifications this fort lasted until it was destroyed by fire around AD105. During its lifetime, probably because the extension of the frontier had overstretched manpower resources, troops were gradually withdrawn from Scotland, first from the forts to the north of the Forth-Clyde isthmus and then from those in the lowlands.

The second fort
Following the destruction of the first fort a new one was built. Its internal buildings were entirely of timber and its plan was similar to that of the first fort. At this time, in the early years of the second century AD, the northern frontier of Britain lay on the neck of land between the Tyne and the Solway. It was not a physical barrier like a wall, but rather what the Roman called a *limes* – a frontier patrol road, linking forts and signalling stations. This system was designed to enable large numbers of troops to move quickly to any trouble spots. The new fort at Corbridge was one

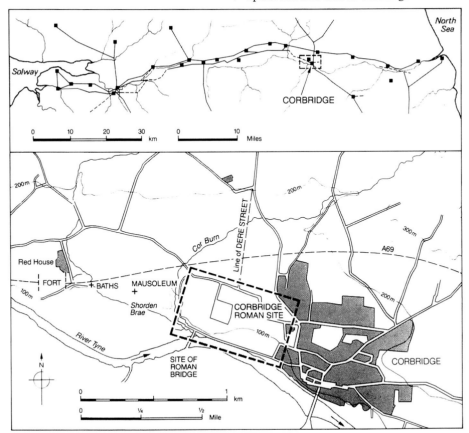

Corbridge Roman Site and surrounding area

20 PLAN

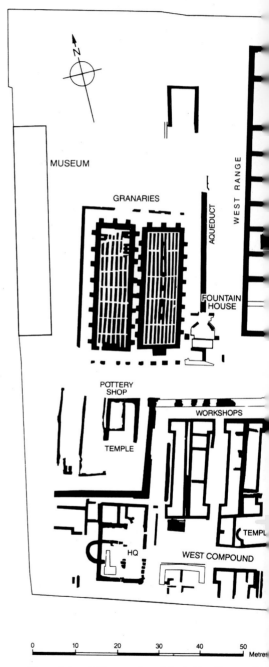

Plan of the visible remains of Corbridge Roman Site

PLAN 21

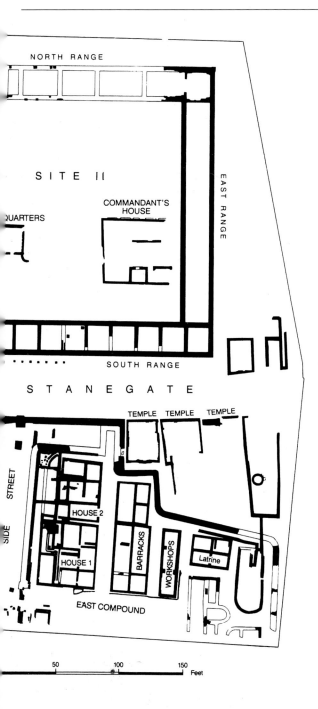

HISTORY: The forts at Corbridge

The god Hercules was much favoured by Roman soldiers. This sculpture, found in the shrine within the headquarters building in the west compound, shows Hercules killing the Hydra (Hydra is on the missing piece of stone), aided by Minerva on the left. The sculpture is now in the museum

of the major forts near its eastern end, controlling a crossing of the river Tyne.

The third fort and Hadrian's Wall

The second fort lasted until about AD120, by which time the policy of the imperial government towards frontiers had changed. Under the emperor Hadrian it was decided to replace the system of forts and roads with a solid frontier, Hadrian's Wall. Initial plans for this involved housing fighting troops well behind the line of the wall itself, and at around this time the fort at Corbridge, some 4 kilometres to the south of the Wall, was rebuilt again, in line with this policy. It was similar in form and layout to the previous two but probably intended for an infantry garrison. Subsequently, however, imperial strategy changed again: new forts were built on the line of the wall itself to accommodate the troops. It was once thought that the third fort at Corbridge must then have been at least partially abandoned, but there is no archaeological evidence to support this.

The last fort

In AD139 the emperor Antoninus Pius decided to attempt once more the occupation of lowland Scotland. The line of the frontier was moved forward and a turf wall, the Antonine Wall, was built across the isthmus between the Forth and the Clyde. Corbridge, being situated on a main road into Scotland, received new buildings and a fresh garrison.

This was the first fort on the site where extensive use was made of stone, though some of the buildings may have carried timber superstructure. Parts of two stone granaries have been located underneath the visible pair. Their inscribed dedication stones were found re-used as paving stones in the later granaries and are now on display in the museum. The name of the governor of Britain of the time, Quintus Lollius Urbicus, appears on them. In front of the fountain the stonework of the south-west corner of a workshop can be seen, and in the courtyard of the building known as Site 11 the commanding officer's house and parts of the back range of rooms within the headquarters building are still visible.

The end of the forts

The Antonine Wall seems to have formed the northern frontier of Britain for only about twenty years. Around AD163 it was abandoned and Hadrian's Wall was recommissioned. This seems to have marked the end of Corbridge as a regular auxiliary fort as there is evidence that the ramparts were levelled at around this

HISTORY: Development of the town

time, and the next major phase of building on the site is of a very different character. With the forts on Hadrian's Wall once more filled with troops, there was presumably no need to maintain a garrison at Corbridge.

Development of the town

Early development

The history of the next fifty or so years is not well understood, but by the early third century the character of the settlement at Corbridge had changed and it had become essentially a town. Like many other Roman towns in Britain its origins were military. The mixed community which had grown up as a result of the trading opportunities provided by the fort formed the basis of the town when the garrison was withdrawn. There was still a military presence, in the form of a small legionary depot, at its heart, but this was probably much smaller and more specialised than the garrison of the fort had been.

The demolition and clearance of the fort does not seem to have been completed immediately after 163 but rather to have been carried out in a piecemeal way over quite a long period of time. Over parts of the levelled east rampart various shed-like timber buildings were erected, and metal-working furnaces were built over both east and west ramparts. Probably at this point also, a number of small, rectangular stone buildings, which may have been temples, were built in the area to the south of the main east-west street. Most of them faced on to this street but one, smaller than the rest and with an apse at its west end, lay on the west side of the intersecting north-south street.

Not long before AD180 building on a

A gaming board, dice, counters and dice shakers, all found at Corbridge, and no doubt used by the garrison

24 HISTORY: Development of the town

larger scale began on the north side of the east-west street. This included a pair of granaries, a fountain house and, to the east of the fountain, the building known as Site 11. Opinions differ as to the purpose of Site 11. Some suggest that it was a forum (the main administrative building of a Roman town) or possibly a market, and that the Roman government of the time was intending to develop Corbridge as a new regional capital. Others maintain that it was a storehouse or workshop complex, in which case it is more likely to have formed part of a military depot. Whichever was the case, the building programme was destined not to be completed in its original form. The later second century was a time of major upheaval in the empire as a whole, with attacks from outside the frontiers occurring along the Rhine and the Danube as well as in northern Britain. Around AD180 a serious disturbance occurred on the northern frontier; Cassius Dio, a historian of the time, says that enemy tribes crossed the frontier, devastated large areas and killed a general and the troops he had with him. They were only brought under control by the special appointment of a particularly skilled and ruthless general called Ulpius Marcellus. At Corbridge extensive burnt deposits have been found which probably came from the destruction of timber buildings and which could date to this time. It is not clear whether the destruction resulted from enemy action or from Roman demolition. Work in progress on the stone buildings was suspended. The granaries and the fountain house were completed later, but Site 11 was almost certainly never completed to its original plan.

Following the destruction, probably around the turn of the second and third centuries, work on the granaries and fountain was completed and new buildings were constructed on the south side of the main street. These were enclosed by thick walls to form two

Site 11, looking east. Building of the main 'courtyard' building is thought to have begun in about AD180, though the remains within the courtyard date from the earlier forts

compounds each with a gate giving access from the side street. It is not clear what all the buildings within the compounds were used for. In the east compound at least two were residential houses. In the west compound some at least were used as workshops and one is thought to have been an administrative block. The buildings which faced directly on to the main street were excluded from the compounds, and from the way in which the compound walls wind their way behind them, these buildings were obviously already in existence when the compound walls were built. The small building with the apse which stood on the west side of the side street was incorporated in the wall and gate of the west compound.

The compounds probably formed part of a military works depot and from inscriptions we know that they were occupied by soldiers of the second and sixth legions. In the early years of the third century the emperor Severus conducted a number of military campaigns in Scotland, and it is likely that the base at Corbridge formed part of the supply network for this army. An altar (on display in the museum) which was set up by an officer in charge of the granaries refers to 'the most successful expedition to Britain'. This was probably the expedition of Severus.

Whether the two compounds served different functions is open to debate. It may be that the east compound was for residential accommodation, while the west compound was used as a workplace. However, the 'workshops' in the west compound might originally have been barracks, and this, together with the presence of residential houses within the east compound, could imply that the west compound provided accommodation for the men, with the east compound for the officers.

This altar was set up by Gaius Julius Apolinaris, the centurion of the sixth legion, which garrisoned Corbridge in the early third century. It is dedicated to Jupiter Dolichenus, Caelestis-Brigantia and Salus, and demonstrates the all-embracing nature of Roman religion. The Roman god Jupiter is identified with the eastern god Dolichenus and associated with the personification of the local Brigantes tribe, which is linked to Juno Caelestis, Jupiter's consort. Salus was the god of personal well-being

The third and fourth centuries

Much less is known of the history of Corbridge in the third and fourth centuries than in the earlier period. The compounds, together with Site 11, the fountain and the granaries, formed the nucleus of the town, while an elaborate house east of Dere Street between the Stanegate and the Tyne bridge may have been the residence for an imperial official. But most of the town lies outside the area on view today, under the surface of the surrounding fields: the known buildings cover an area of about 27 acres (11 ha). The official buildings at the centre of the town were clearly surrounded by houses, for the most part simple rectangular structures, with their ends fronting on to the street. These may have served as shops or workshops and living quarters alike: many of them may have had upper storeys and housed the wealthier merchants, while others were occupied by artisans - such as leather workers, potters and smiths. Such houses lined the Stanegate and Dere Street some distance from the centre of the town, and elsewhere were connected with these main roads by other roads or lanes on a roughly rectangular layout.

The town no doubt depended for its prosperity on servicing the troops along Hadrian's Wall, for whom its temples and shops may have made it an attractive leave-centre. Other sources of wealth would have been the minerals which then as now were mined in the surrounding district (lead, iron and coal), the corn which filled its granaries, and trade with the local population.

We can only piece together fragments of the history of the town in this period from archaeological evidence. Although the whole of Site 11 was never completed in its original form, the rooms of the south range, and the south end of the west range, were used throughout the

third century and well into the fourth. A portico was added outside the west end of the south range. At some point, probably in the third century, the compounds were united by a wall which was built across the north end of the side street, and many of the buildings inside were modified or extended. Several coin hoards dating to around the middle of the fourth century were found in the area around the fountain. They are more likely to be the result of currency devaluations and government regulations of the time, than the sign of some disaster. Somewhat later there was a fire in a small building outside the north-west corner of the west compound. From the large amounts of pottery found in the

HISTORY: Corbridge after the Romans   27

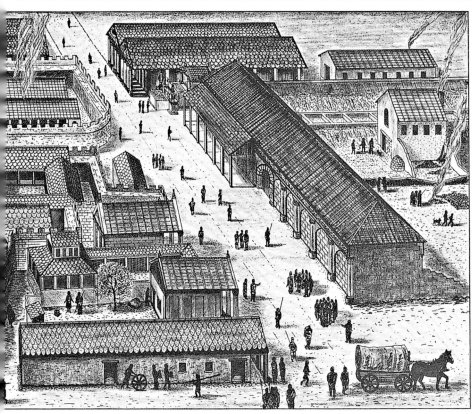

A reconstruction of Corbridge as it may have appeared in the early third century, looking west down the main street. Construction of the courtyard building (right) is under way, and the two compounds south of the street have not yet been linked

burnt debris the building would seem to have been some kind of pottery store, and it has become known as the 'pottery shop'. The pottery dates to the second and third centuries but a group of coins (which seemed to be associated with the debris) suggests a date for the fire of not earlier than AD367. The main street of the town received its last resurfacing not earlier than the middle of the fourth century and coin evidence suggests that the town was occupied until at least the end of the fourth century.

Corbridge after the Romans

Whether the Roman site at Corbridge was eventually abandoned, and if so when, can only be a matter for speculation. In 396 some reorganisation of the British frontier is recorded by the poet Claudian. In 407 the British army chose their own emperor, Constantine, who departed for the Continent to try to win the imperial throne, and may have taken troops with him. Britain became cut off from the rest of the empire and rule from Rome was never restored. The town at Corbridge might have survived, perhaps with some sort of local authority, beyond the end of the fourth century, but whether it was still inhabited when the first Anglian settlers came to Corbridge has not been revealed by excavation.

Rediscovery and excavation

There was an excavation, in search of treasure, at Corbridge, as early as 1201, in the reign of King John. 'Nothing was found' recorded the chronicler Roger de Hoveden, 'except stones marked with bronze and iron and lead'. The antiquaries John Leland and William Camden visited Corbridge in the sixteenth century, and were struck by the abundance of the remains; but John Horsley, early in the eighteenth century, noted that the Roman site was almost entirely levelled and under the plough. In fact it had long been used as a quarry, and Hexham Priory, Corbridge parish church and many other buildings had drawn upon its convenient supply of building stone.

In the early nineteenth century the buildings in the south-west quarter of the site, which was the property of the Duke of Northumberland, were largely removed 'to promote agricultural improvements', and a number of discoveries resulted. In 1861-62 some digging by William Coulson uncovered the north abutment of the Roman bridge and other structures, including part of a baths, inside the town. But it was not until the establishment of a special excavation committee, under the auspices of the Northumberland County History Committee, that systematic excavation began. Excavations in 1906-14 resulted in the recovery of the greater part of the plan of the town, and of a large collection of sculpture, inscriptions, coins, pottery and small objects. In 1933 the central part of the site, containing the most important buildings discovered in 1906-14, was placed in the care of the Ancient Monuments Department. This area has subsequently become the focus of archaeological work on the site.

From 1934, apart from the war years, an annual excavation season took place on the site until 1973; a further small excavation took place in 1976, and the area west of the visible granaries was examined in 1980 before the new museum was built. This systematic investigation has shed some light in particular on the history and layout of the sequence of forts on the Corbridge site.

THE MUSEUM

The many seasons of excavation on the site have produced a wealth of finds. The best examples of these have been used in the museum display to tell the story of Roman Corbridge and to give some insight into the way the inhabitants of the forts and town lived their lives.

The display is arranged in a clockwise sequence. The first half concentrates on the history of the site and is arranged next to the large windows which overlook the remains. Each section deals with a separate period of the site's history and is accompanied by a case of objects which would have been in use at the time. In the second half of the display, each section is related to a particular aspect of life in Roman Corbridge, such as trade, domestic life and religious observance.

Note on dating

Many of the objects provide valuable information about the date of the archaeological layers in which they were found. Inscriptions, coins and pottery are particularly useful in this respect.

Roman **inscriptions** were written in an abbreviated form of Latin. The form of official inscriptions was quite standard so it is often possible to restore an inscription from a small fragment. Official inscriptions usually mention the name of the emperor and often the name of the governor of Britain also, and these can be used to date the inscription. Some or all of the emperor's titles are usually mentioned. Since an emperor may have taken a particular title in a specific year this can provide a very close date. Some titles, such as Consul *(COS)* and Tribunician Power *(TR P)*, were awarded more than once, and the number of times the title had been awarded is given with the abbreviated title, such as *III COS* – Consul for the third time. This can also provide a very close date for an inscription.

Coinage in gold, silver and bronze was produced at a number of mints in the Roman empire. The size and weight of the different denominations varied quite considerably at different times. The two faces of a coin are known as the obverse and the reverse. The obverse of a coin carried the emperor's portrait with a legend around the edge, giving his name and titles. The reverse was used by the Roman government as a sort of billboard to promote its policies, and a wide range of reverse types and legends was used. Among the more popular were godlike personifications such as *Libertas* (Liberty), *Fortuna* (Luck or Good Fortune) and *Providentia* (Providence), with legends like *Libertas Publica* (Public Liberty), *Fortuna Redux* (Good Fortune Restored) and *Providentia Augusti* (the Providence of the Emperor). Size and weight alone will usually give a general indication of date, and coins of certain periods, in good condition, can often be closely dated.

The **pottery** found on northern military sites like Corbridge came from a wide variety of sources. Some was imported from other parts of the empire but most was produced within the province. The main imported type was samian, a fine table-ware with a glossy red surface. The samian found at Corbridge was produced in three places: South, Central and East Gaul. South Gaulish samian dates mostly to the first century AD, Central Gaulish to the second century AD and East Gaulish to the later second and third centuries AD. Samian was produced in a number of standard shapes which have been classified by scholars: Dragendorff's classification is the most used, and the type numbers of his system are preceded by the abbreviation of his name, 'Dr'. Certain of the shapes (principally Dr 29 and 37) were decorated in relief. These bowls were produced by being thrown in a mould whose inner face carried a stamped impression of the decorative scheme. In this way a large number of bowls could be produced from one mould. Both the potters and the mould-makers signed their names on their products. By amassing and comparing information on the different stamps and decorative schemes it has been possible to classify the work of both workshops and individual potters. As a result a decorated samian vessel can often be attributed, with some confidence, to a specific potter, and dated to within quite a narrow margin.

Most of the coarser, domestic pottery was produced at a number of centres in Britain. Certain types have been recognised on sites all over the country and enough is now known about their origin and development for them to be used as reliable dating tools. One such type is called Black Burnished Ware and it occurs in two varieties (usually abbreviated BB1 and BB2). BB1 was produced in Dorset and the Midlands and first arrived at sites like Corbridge around AD120. BB2 was produced in Kent and Essex and first arrived in the north around AD140. BBl continued to be supplied to the north until the end of the third century but BB2 was probably not supplied after the middle of the century. In the fourth century much of the pottery in use in the north came from a large industry in Yorkshire, which supplied a wide range of vessels including a distinctive kind of cooking-pot in a black calcite-gritted fabric.

Mortaria (grit-studded mixing bowls) are another type of vessel which provide valuable dating evidence. They were vessels of specialised function used in food preparation which took considerable skill to manufacture. Up until the end of the second century the potters making mortaria stamped them either with an abbreviated form of their name or with a trade mark (often a leaf). As with samian, careful study of the stamps and their distribution has enabled many of the production centres to be identified and the work of certain potters to be dated quite closely.

This splendid example of a 'Hunt' cup came from a large pottery industry in the Nene valley, near modern Peterborough (see page 38)

History

The Agricolan supply base at Red House
The objects in this case are all of first-century date and were recovered during the excavations of the Agricolan supply base at Red House in 1974. The coin (15) is a silver denarius of the emperor Vespasian, dating to AD74. The samian was produced in South Gaul. Fragments of decorated bowls of form Dr 29 (a ridged or carinated bowl – no 1) and form Dr 37 (a hemispherical bowl – no 2) were found. The mortaria (19) were also imported from Gaul. The larger one bears the stamp of its maker Cacumattus. The gemstone (16) is made of chalcedony (a kind of quartz) and shows a figure of the god Mars carrying a trophy. The brooches (8) would have been worn as a pair linked by the chains. The hipposandal (6) was a form of temporary horseshoe common in Roman Gaul and Britain.

The forts at Corbridge I
The first fort at Corbridge is slightly later in date than that at Red House, though the pottery from the two sites is very similar. The decoration of the samian bowl (14) is typical of the period AD60-80. The small mortarium (17), which carries the stamp of its maker Gaius Atisius Sabinus, was imported from Gaul. The cooking pot with the rusticated surface (11), the three carinated bowls (1) and the lamp are typical of the late first century. The garrison of the earliest fort is thought to have been cavalry. Many of the other objects in the case (3, 4, 8, 9 and 16) have obvious associations with horses.

Next to the case is a replica of the tombstone of Flavinus, a standard-bearer of the Ala Petriana which is thought to have been the first garrison at Corbridge. The original was found at Hexham Abbey. The tombstone depicts Flavinus on horseback riding over the body of an enemy warrior.

The Corbridge hoard
In 1964 archaeologists uncovered the remains of a wooden chest in the south-east corner of Site 11, one of the most significant discoveries from Roman Britain. The chest had been made of alder wood, strengthened at its corners and covered in leather for waterproofing. It seems to have been buried during the earlier part of the second century AD, possibly for safe storage while its owner was posted elsewhere. Inside was a mix of tools, scrap material, personal items, weapons and, most importantly, sections of *loricae segmentatae* – Roman segmental armour. These contents may be a miscellaneous collection from a workshop, possessions in need of repair, or simply a reserve stock of material kept as spares or to be reworked as new equipment. Many of these items are on display here; others are in the Great North Museum, Newcastle upon Tyne. The following list gives some idea of the richness of the find:

Armour: parts of at least six cuirasses of plate armour (*loricae segmentatae*).
Weapons: pila, bundles of spearheads, catapult bolts, ferrules.
Tools and Implements: pickaxe, saw, shears, crow bar, knife, pulley block, lamp and bracket, hinges, bowl, key.
Fittings/Miscellaneous: hooks, chest fittings, nail, scabbard, belt plate, furniture fittings, gaming counters, melon beads, window glass, whetstones, tankard, and fragments of writing tablets, papyrus, textile and rope.

The forts at Corbridge II
In the early years of the second century the fort was rebuilt. By this time most of

the samian imported into Britain was coming from central rather than southern Gaul. In decorated ware the hemispherical bowl form Dr 37 had completely replaced the more complex carinated form Dr 29. One of the Dr 37 bowls in this case was signed by the potter Butrio (1). The small cup (form Dr 33, no 14) was first produced in the first century but became most popular in the second century. The open dishes (Dr 18/31, nos 13 and 15) had developed from shallower first-century forms (Dr 18). They bear the stamps of the potters Granio and Muxtullus. Coarseware of BB 1 type (9, 11 and 12; see note on dating) seems to have been introduced into northern Britain around AD120 when the building of Hadrian's Wall started. The metalwork in the case is almost exclusively military. The artillery bolts (5), arrowheads (6), spear butts and spearheads (7 and 8) could well have stocked an armoury in the fort at this period.

The forts at Corbridge III

The fort was rebuilt again at about the time when the building of the Antonine Wall started. The decoration on the samian bowl (14) is typical of this period. One of the small cups (17) (Dr 33) is stamped by Banuus. The deep bowl (19) (Dr 31) is stamped by Albillus. This kind of bowl developed from the earlier, shallower bowls of forms Dr 18/31. Vessels in BB2 (2, 3, 15 and 16; see note on dating) began arriving in the north around AD140. The 'poppy-head' beaker decorated with bands of dots (8) came from the same area (Kent and Essex) as the vessels in BB2. The small beaker (1) has a 'rough-cast' surface. The mortarium (5) has a trade-mark in the form of a leaf stamped on it.

Inscriptions and sculpture

The two inscriptions next to the window were found re-used as paving slabs in the floors of the two granaries. They are thought to have come from earlier granaries whose remains lie under the visible pair. They were both set up by the second legion (titled Augusta), and both mention the emperor Antoninus Pius. One inscription is dated AD139 when Antoninus Pius was in his second consulship (*II COS*) and the other dates to AD140, his third consulship (*III COS*). Both mention the name of the governor at the time, Quintus Lollius Urbicus.

Next to them is a stone bearing a sculptured relief of a Victory who rests her left foot on a globe and holds a large griffin-headed *pelta* (a shield) in both hands. Reliefs like this were often used on either side of large dedicatory inscriptions like those just mentioned, giving the impression that the inscription was being carried by the two flying Victories.

Against the wall is a very fine inscription which is likely to have come from a temple. The god, Sol Invictus (the unconquered sun), is mentioned in the first line. This was erased in Roman times, probably because of a mistaken connection with the damned emperor Elegabalus who was a devotee of the cult of Sol Invictus. After his death in AD222 he was officially discredited (the modern Latin term is *damnatio memoriae*) and his name was removed from all official inscriptions.

Next to this is a large dedication slab which was reconstructed from fragments found both on the site and in Corbridge village. It is dedicated to the emperors Marcus Aurelius and Lucius Verus who ruled jointly between AD161 and 169. The details of their titles enable the inscription to be dated to the autumn of

The Corbridge lion, probably originally carved as a grave ornament, and later re-used as a fountain head

AD 163. The inscription was set up by the twentieth legion (titled Valeria Victrix) and mentions the governor of the time, Sextus Calpurnius Agricola.

Close by is a large and well-carved base, probably from a statue, carrying a dedication to the Discipline of the Emperors. It was found on the steps of the underground strong room of the headquarters building of the west compound and probably came from the regimental shrine.

Across from the statue base is an altar found inside the south entrance of the west granary. The inscription mentions the granaries (*horreorum*) and seems to have been set up by an officer who was in charge of them (*praepositus curam agens*

horreorum) at the time of the campaigns of the Emperor Severus in northern Britain (*tempore expeditionis felicissimae Brittannicae*).

Next to the altar are some of the fragments of the ornamental pediment of the fountain house (see page 8). The accompanying drawing shows how it would have looked originally.

In the middle of this area is a model showing a portion of the site as it might have looked towards the end of the second century AD when construction of the large courtyard building (Site 11) had started. Although the part shown in the model may have been completed and used, the whole building was never finished.

MUSEUM: Life in Roman Corbridge

The later military occupation

This case contains a small selection of the large number of items of third- and fourth-century date recovered from the site. The bronze cheek piece (10), which has recently been restored, is from a cavalry sports helmet. The helmet handles (15) are in the shape of a pair of opposed dolphins. The bronze openwork mount (23) contains a fragmentary inscription – *COH(ors) OPT(imi) MAX(imi)* – meaning 'The cohort of all-powerful Jupiter'. The pottery includes examples of colour-coated beakers made in the Nene Valley near Peterborough (1–4, 11), and a large moulded beaker with rouletted decoration, which was probably imported from Gaul (12). By the fourth century much of northern Britain was being supplied with pottery from Yorkshire. The dish (7), cooking pots (5 and 13), flanged bowl (6), and shallow painted dish (8) are all examples of this (13 and 6 are modern reproductions). The curved roof-tile (14) would have fitted over the flanges of two adjoining flat tiles. It carries the stamp of the sixth legion (Victrix).

The Corbridge lion

The sculpture of a lion crouching over a dead stag was probably originally carved as a grave monument. Later a hole was cut through the lion's mouth and it was re-used as an ornamental fountain head. It was found in the filling of a cistern in a building to the south of the west compound. There seems to have been a workshop at Corbridge producing these monuments, as another is known from the site and one was found in the excavations of a Roman mausoleum at Shorden Brae close by.

On the wall behind the lion is a plan showing the extent of the Roman town. Since it was compiled in 1982 more buildings have been revealed by aerial photography.

Life in Roman Corbridge

Personal effects

Most of the items in this case would have been worn about the person. The bronze purse (1) was worn on the arm; another example is known from the fort at South Shields. The collection of brooches from the site is particularly fine, and a selection is shown here (16–18, 36–44). Of the gemstones found on the site those included here are among the best examples. No 48 is in red jasper (a kind of opaque quartz, the colour being due to particles of iron oxide) and shows a design combining an elephant head and a mask of the god Silenus. Nos 49 and 50 are in nicolo paste (artificial onyx). No 49 shows a horse and no 50 shows the figure of a huntsman wearing a tunic and carrying a large animal over his shoulder and another in his right hand. No 51 is in dark chalcedony (a kind of quartz) and shows a rhinoceros tethered to a tree.

Building in the Roman town

In a settlement of the size of Corbridge there was probably always some kind of building work in progress somewhere. The case contains some of the tools which would have been used. Some of them (such as the hammers, the trowel and the chisels – nos 11–14 and 16–17)

Gem from a ring depicting a rhinoceros tethered to a tree

are strikingly similar to ones in use today. On the wall to the right of the case is a selection of column capitals which show the skill of the local stonemasons.

Local industry and pottery
As a town Corbridge would have been a centre of local industry where craftsmen of many kinds could work and trade. At least four potters who made mortaria are thought to have worked at Corbridge. One of the name stamps used by Saturninus is shown here together with a vessel which carries an impression of the stamp (6). There are vessels stamped by

This glass flask, with handles shaped like dolphins, would have contained bath oils

Sulloniacus (10) and Cudrenus (11). There was also a potter, or potters, making grey-ware vessels decorated with figures in relief (nos 1–5). No 3 is a clay mould for a figure, possibly intended to be a god, accompanied by a wheel. No 5 shows a figure of a smith; on the anvil and under the figure's feet is a name, Assetio. The small crucibles (12) were probably for bronze. Extensive metal-working, both of iron and bronze, is known to have taken place on the site. The awls (14) and needles (15 and 16) were used in working leather. The bronze needle (16) is shown with a modern steel needle for comparison. The iron tools in the bottom right-hand side of the case (17–24) would all have been used in working wood.

Glass
Most of the glass vessels found at the site would have come from the Rhineland but a few pieces such as the fragment of millefiore glass (1) and the cast and

A depiction of a Celtic god on a plaque made from a pottery mould found at Corbridge

polished bowls (2) may have come from Italy or even Alexandria. The piller-moulded bowls (so-called because of the decoration of vertical 'pillers') are characteristic of the late first century (3). The large flask with the triangular body (6) is almost complete: it dates to the late first or second century. In the later second and third centuries a workshop in Cologne was supplying northern Britain with a particularly distinctive small cylindrical bowl decorated with painted arena scenes (15). Similar small bowls engraved with fishes and sometimes letters and palm-branches (16) may have come from the same workshop. The small flask (28) was found in a mid second-century pit. It has handles in the shape of dolphins. These flasks are direct copies of bronze flasks for carrying bathing oils and are frequently found with an attached set of strigils (small scrapers used for scraping the body clean in the hot, steamy atmosphere of the baths).

Domestic life

In the right-hand case, the stone gaming board (1 – see page 23) marked out in squares is likely to have been used for a game like draughts. Bone was a favourite material for making and accompanying counters, dice and dice-shakers, but counters were often also made out of cut-down fragments of pottery. Light was

An oil-lamp typical of the kind found at Corbridge

mostly provided by wax candles, tapers or oil-lamps (12–14). A variety of candle-sticks is shown here (8, 10, 11); no 10 is a fine example in bronze with enamel decoration. Permanent written records were made in ink on papyrus or thin tablets of wood, and wax tablets, which could be re-used many times, were also used. Non-spill inkwells in samian (16) are quite common. Next to them are writing styli of bone and iron (17) resting on a modern reproduction of a wood and wax writing tablet.

The lock mechanisms (15) in the left-hand case were quite sophisticated. Keys were made in bronze (4) or iron (18). Some were meant to be carried on the person and had handles in the shape of a ring. A variety of latches, handles, hooks and chains (17, 19, 20 and 21) would have been used to secure doors, windows and lids. A selection of iron knives, some with bone handles, is also shown (9–11). The fine bronze jug (23) was found in a pit to the west of the site.

MUSEUM: Imports to Corbridge   37

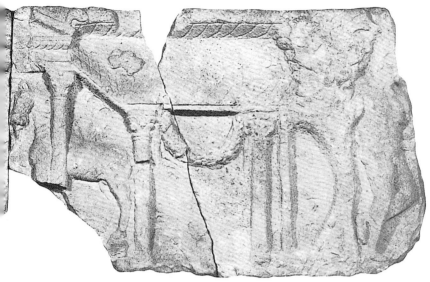

Frieze from a temple dedicated to Jupiter Dolichenus, showing the sun god (left) riding towards the house of one of the heavenly twins, Castor or Pollux, who is leading a horse. Sculptures like this show how richly ornamented the buildings at Corbridge would have been

A bronze jug, found to the west of the site

Imports to Corbridge
Much of the fine pottery found on the site was imported from the continent. The beakers with the dark, lustrous surface (5) came from Germany, while the samian came from a number of centres in Gaul. No 10 – a bowl of form Dr 29 – came from south Gaul. The cup (6, form Dr 33 stamped by Albucius) and the beaker (8) came from central Gaul, as did bowls 12 (form Dr 31 stamped by the potter Genitor) and 1 (form 37 stamped by Cinnamus); the workshop of Cinnamus was the most prolific of the later second century. Nos 2, 9 (form Dr 37), 7 (beaker) and 11 (form Dr 38) came from a number of centres in east Gaul. Throughout the Roman period large quantities of olive oil and wine were imported into Britain and fragments of the containers (amphorae) are often found. No 3 is the neck and shoulder of a large globular olive oil amphora from

MUSEUM: Religion

The tombstone of a baby girl, Vellibia, which depicts a child holding a ball as if in play

Spain; no 4 is a fragment from a much smaller vessel (known as a 'carrot' amphora since the shape and colour are reminiscent of a carrot) which possibly contained figs or dates.

Agriculture and trade

Some of the objects found on the site did not come from so far afield. The cups and beakers (1) came from a large pottery industry in the Nene valley near modern Peterborough. Many of the cups (known as 'Hunt' cups) show scenes of dogs chasing rabbits and other animals. The pestles and mortars (3 and 5) are made of Purbeck marble and came from southern Britain. A number of objects associated with spinning and weaving are shown: a distaff and spindle (9), spindle whorls (10), weaving combs of bone and antler (13) and a weaving tablet of bone (11). The collection of surgical and medical instruments (2a–i) is one of the largest single groups found in Britain. It contains handles from scalpels and surgical knives, forceps, and a variety of sounds, probes and ointment scoops (*ligulae*).

Religion

There is evidence from the rich variety of religious objects found on the site for a number of well-appointed shrines or temples. One was dedicated to Roma Aeterna (Eternal Rome) and sculptured panels from it were found in the latest level of the main east-west street. They show a faun and nymph among vine tendrils. Another was dedicated to Jupiter Dolichenus, whose cult spread across the empire from Doliche in Asia Minor. Fragments of the temple frieze were found. They show, on the right, Apollo, in the centre, one of the heavenly twins (Castor and Pollux) leading a horse, and, on the left, Sol (the sun god) riding a winged horse. An altar to Jupiter

Dolichenus who also found, dedicated by Gaius Julius Apolinaris, a centurion of the sixth legion (see page 25).

One of the finest objects is the silver dish known as the Corbridge *Lanx*, of which a replica is shown in the central case in the rear gallery (the original is in the British Museum). It was found on the banks of the river Tyne close to the site, and is probably of late fourth-century date. The main field of the dish shows Apollo in his sanctuary on Delos, attended by Athena and Artemis.

Other objects, such as the relief of the three mother goddesses (*matres*), and many of the stone heads, have more affinities with the Celtic element of religious belief in Roman Britain.

The evidence from the site for Christianity is only slight. A gold betrothal ring inscribed *Aemilia Zeses* ('Long life to Aemilia' – *Zeses* has possible Christian connotations) is known from the site (a replica is displayed in the 'Personal effects' case). The decoration of fishes and palm-leaves engraved on fragments of glass (see the Glass case) may have had Christian significance.

Death

The display concludes with some of the gravestones found on the site. One is that of a *vexillum* (flag) bearer called Barathes from Palmyra (in modern Syria). He was 68 when he died and he may be the same man who set up a tombstone to his wife Regina at South Shields. The two best preserved gravestones from the site are of children. Ahtehe the daughter of Nobilis was only five when she died and Vellibia Ertola (Ertola may have been her nickname) was even younger. Vellibia's tombstone shows a figure holding a small object (maybe a ball) as if in play.

The Corbridge Lanx